HOMESTEAD COOKBOOK

**MEGA BUNDLE – 4 Manuscripts in 1 –
160+ Homestead - friendly recipes
including pie, cookie, and smoothies for a
delicious and tasty diet**

TABLE OF CONTENTS

Introduction

Homestead recipes for personal enjoyment but also for family enjoyment. You will love them for sure for how easy it is to prepare them.

BREAKFAST

BANANA PANCAKES

Serves: **4**

Prep Time: **10**   Minutes

Cook Time: **20**   Minutes

Total Time: **30**   Minutes

INGREDIENTS

- 1 cup whole wheat flour
- ¼ tsp baking soda
- ¼ tsp baking powder
- 1 cup banana
- 2 eggs
- 1 cup milk

DIRECTIONS

1. In a bowl combine all ingredients together and mix well
2. In a skillet heat olive oil
3. Pour ¼ of the batter and cook each pancake for 1-2 minutes per side
4. When ready remove from heat and serve

ALMOND PANCAKES

Serves: **4**

Prep Time: **10**   Minutes

Cook Time: **30**   Minutes

Total Time: **40**   Minutes

INGREDIENTS

- 1 cup whole wheat flour
- ¼ tsp baking soda
- ¼ tsp baking powder
- 1 cup almonds
- 2 eggs
- 1 cup milk

DIRECTIONS

1. In a bowl combine all ingredients together and mix well
2. In a skillet heat olive oil
3. Pour ¼ of the batter and cook each pancake for 1-2 minutes per side
4. When ready remove from heat and serve

APRICOTS PANCAKES

Serves: **4**

Prep Time: **10**   Minutes

Cook Time: **20**   Minutes

Total Time: **30**   Minutes

INGREDIENTS

- 1 cup whole wheat flour
- ¼ tsp baking soda
- ¼ tsp baking powder
- 1 cup mashed apricots
- 2 eggs
- 1 cup milk

DIRECTIONS

1. In a bowl combine all ingredients together and mix well
2. In a skillet heat olive oil
3. Pour ¼ of the batter and cook each pancake for 1-2 minutes per side
4. When ready remove from heat and serve

STRAWBERRY PANCAKES

Serves: *4*
Prep Time: *10* Minutes

Cook Time: *20* Minutes

Total Time: *30* Minutes

INGREDIENTS

-   1 cup whole wheat flour
-   ¼ tsp baking soda
-   ¼ tsp baking powder
-   1 cup strawberries
-   2 eggs
-   1 cup milk

DIRECTIONS

1. In a bowl combine all ingredients together and mix well
2. In a skillet heat olive oil
3. Pour ¼ of the batter and cook each pancake for 1-2 minutes per side
4. When ready remove from heat and serve

Serves: **4**

Prep Time: **10** Minutes

Cook Time: **30** Minutes

Total Time: **40** Minutes

INGREDIENTS

- 1 cup whole wheat flour
- ¼ tsp baking soda
- ¼ tsp baking powder
- 2 eggs
- 1 cup milk
- 1 cup blackberries

DIRECTIONS

1. In a bowl combine all ingredients together and mix well
2. In a skillet heat olive oil
3. Pour ¼ of the batter and cook each pancake for 1-2 minutes per side
4. When ready remove from heat and serve

GINGERBREAD MUFFINS

Serves: *8-12*

Prep Time: *10*   Minutes

Cook Time: *20*   Minutes

Total Time: *30*   Minutes

INGREDIENTS

- 2 eggs
- 1 tablespoon olive oil
- 1 cup milk
- 2 cups whole wheat flour
- 1 tsp baking soda
- ¼ tsp baking soda
- 1 tsp ginger
- 1 tsp cinnamon
- ¼ cup molasses

DIRECTIONS

1. In a bowl combine all wet ingredients
2. In another bowl combine all dry ingredients
3. Combine wet and dry ingredients together
4. Fold in ginger and mix well
5. Pour mixture into 8-12 prepared muffin cups, fill 2/3 of the cups

6. Bake for 18-20 minutes at 375 F
7. When ready remove from the oven and serve

DATE MUFFINS

Serves: *8-12*

Prep Time: *10*   Minutes

Cook Time: *20*   Minutes

Total Time: *30*   Minutes

INGREDIENTS

- 2 eggs
- 1 tablespoon olive oil
- 1 cup milk
- 2 cups whole wheat flour
- 1 tsp baking soda
- ¼ tsp baking soda
- 1 tsp cinnamon
- ½ cup dates

DIRECTIONS

1. In a bowl combine all wet ingredients
2. In another bowl combine all dry ingredients
3. Combine wet and dry ingredients together
4. Pour mixture into 8-12 prepared muffin cups, fill 2/3 of the cups
5. Bake for 18-20 minutes at 375 F
6. When ready remove from the oven and serve

BLUEBERRY MUFFINS

Serves:	*8-12*	
Prep Time:	*10*	Minutes
Cook Time:	*20*	Minutes
Total Time:	*30*	Minutes

INGREDIENTS

- 2 eggs
- 1 tablespoon olive oil
- 1 cup milk
- 2 cups whole wheat flour
- 1 tsp baking soda
- ¼ tsp baking soda
- 1 tsp cinnamon
- 1 cup blueberries

DIRECTIONS

1. In a bowl combine all wet ingredients
2. In another bowl combine all dry ingredients
3. Combine wet and dry ingredients together
4. Fold in blueberries and mix well
5. Pour mixture into 8-12 prepared muffin cups, fill 2/3 of the cups
6. Bake for 18-20 minutes at 375F

CANTALOUPE MUFFINS

Serves: *8-12*

Prep Time: *10*   Minutes

Cook Time: *20*   Minutes

Total Time: *30*   Minutes

INGREDIENTS

- 2 eggs
- 1 tablespoon olive oil
- 1 cup milk
- 2 cups whole wheat flour
- 1 tsp baking soda
- ¼ tsp baking soda
- 1 tsp cinnamon
- 1 cup cantaloupe

DIRECTIONS

1. In a bowl combine all wet ingredients
2. In another bowl combine all dry ingredients
3. Combine wet and dry ingredients together
4. Pour mixture into 8-12 prepared muffin cups, fill 2/3 of the cups
5. Bake for 18-20 minutes at 375 F
6. When ready remove from the oven and serve

CRANBERRIES MUFFINS

Serves: *8-12*

Prep Time: *10*   Minutes

Cook Time: *20*   Minutes

Total Time: *30*   Minutes

INGREDIENTS

-   2 eggs
-   1 tablespoon olive oil
-   1 cup milk
-   2 cups whole wheat flour
-   1 tsp baking soda
-   ¼ tsp baking soda
-   1 tsp cinnamon
-   1 cup cranberries

DIRECTIONS

1. In a bowl combine all wet ingredients
2. In another bowl combine all dry ingredients
3. Combine wet and dry ingredients together
4. Pour mixture into 8-12 prepared muffin cups, fill 2/3 of the cups
5. Bake for 18-20 minutes at 375 F
6. When ready remove from the oven and serve

COCONUT MUFFINS

Serves: *8-12*

Prep Time: *10*   Minutes

Cook Time: *20*   Minutes

Total Time: *30*   Minutes

INGREDIENTS

- 2 eggs
- 1 tablespoon olive oil
- 1 cup milk
- 2 cups whole wheat flour
- 1 tsp baking soda
- ¼ tsp baking soda
- 1 tsp cinnamon
- 1 cup coconut flakes

DIRECTIONS

1. In a bowl combine all wet ingredients
2. In another bowl combine all dry ingredients
3. Combine wet and dry ingredients together
4. Pour mixture into 8-12 prepared muffin cups, fill 2/3 of the cups
5. Bake for 18-20 minutes at 375 F
6. When ready remove from the oven and serve

OMELETTE

Serves: *1*
Prep Time: 5   Minutes

Cook Time: **10**   Minutes

Total Time: *15*   Minutes

INGREDIENTS

- 2 eggs
- ¼ tsp salt
- ¼ tsp black pepper
- 1 tablespoon olive oil
- ¼ cup cheese
- ¼ tsp basil
- 1 cup cooked chicken breast

DIRECTIONS

1. In a bowl combine all ingredients together and mix well
2. In a skillet heat olive oil and pour the egg mixture
3. Cook for 1-2 minutes per side
4. When ready remove omelette from the skillet and serve

Serves: *1*
Prep Time: *5*   Minutes

Cook Time: *10*   Minutes

Total Time: *15*   Minutes

INGREDIENTS

- 2 eggs
- ¼ tsp salt
- ¼ tsp black pepper
- 1 tablespoon olive oil
- ¼ cup cheese
- ¼ tsp basil
- 1 cup pumpkin puree
- 1 cup cooked chicken breast

DIRECTIONS

1. In a bowl combine all ingredients together and mix well
2. In a skillet heat olive oil and pour the egg mixture
3. Cook for 1-2 minutes per side
4. When ready remove omelette from the skillet and serve

SNOW PEAS OMELETTE

Serves: **1**
Prep Time: **5**   Minutes
Cook Time: **10** Minutes
Total Time: **15** Minutes

INGREDIENTS

- 2 eggs
- ¼ tsp salt
- ¼ tsp black pepper
- 1 tablespoon olive oil
- ¼ cup cheese
- ¼ tsp basil
- 1 cup chicken breast
- ½ cup snow peas

DIRECTIONS

1. In a bowl combine all ingredients together and mix well
2. In a skillet heat olive oil and pour the egg mixture
3. Cook for 1-2 minutes per side
4. When ready remove omelette from the skillet and serve

MUSHROOM OMELETTE

Serves: **1**
Prep Time: **5**   Minutes

Cook Time: **10**   Minutes

Total Time: **15**   Minutes

INGREDIENTS

- 2 eggs
- ¼ tsp salt
- ¼ tsp black pepper
- 1 tablespoon olive oil
- ¼ cup cheese
- 1 cup turkey breast
- ¼ tsp basil
- 1 cup mushrooms

DIRECTIONS

1. In a bowl combine all ingredients together and mix well
2. In a skillet heat olive oil and pour the egg mixture
3. Cook for 1-2 minutes per side
4. When ready remove omelette from the skillet and serve

Serves: **1**
Prep Time: **5**   Minutes

Cook Time: **10**   Minutes

Total Time: **15**   Minutes

INGREDIENTS

- 2 eggs
- ¼ tsp salt
- ¼ tsp black pepper
- 1 tablespoon olive oil
- ¼ cup cheese
- 1 cup turkey breast
- ¼ tsp basil
- ½ cup radishes

DIRECTIONS

1. In a bowl combine all ingredients together and mix well
2. In a skillet heat olive oil and pour the egg mixture
3. Cook for 1-2 minutes per side
4. When ready remove omelette from the skillet and serve

BEANS OMELETTE

Serves: **1**

Prep Time: **5**   Minutes

Cook Time: **10**   Minutes

Total Time: **15**   Minutes

INGREDIENTS

- 2 eggs
- ¼ tsp salt
- ¼ tsp black pepper
- 1 tablespoon olive oil
- ¼ cup cheese
- ¼ tsp basil
- 1 cup beans

DIRECTIONS

1. In a bowl combine all ingredients together and mix well
2. In a skillet heat olive oil and pour the egg mixture
3. Cook for 1-2 minutes per side
4. When ready remove omelette from the skillet and serve

BREAKFAST GRANOLA

Serves: 2
Prep Time: 5   Minutes

Cook Time: *30*   Minutes

Total Time: *35*   Minutes

INGREDIENTS

- 1 tsp vanilla extract
- 1 tablespoon honey
- 1 lb. rolled oats
- 2 tablespoons sesame seeds
- ¼ lb. almonds
- ¼ lb. berries

DIRECTIONS

1. Preheat the oven to 325 F
2. Spread the granola onto a baking sheet
3. Bake for 12-15 minutes, remove and mix everything
4. Bake for another 12-15 minutes or until slightly brown
5. When ready remove from the oven and serve

RAISIN BREAKFAST MIX

Serves: *1*
Prep Time: 5   Minutes

Cook Time: 5   Minutes

Total Time: *10* Minutes

INGREDIENTS

- ½ cup dried raisins
- ½ cup dried pecans
- ¼ cup almonds
- 1 cup coconut milk
- 1 tsp cinnamon

DIRECTIONS

1. In a bowl combine all ingredients together
2. Serve with milk

Serves: *2*
Prep Time: *5*   Minutes

Cook Time: *15*   Minutes

Total Time: *20*   Minutes

INGREDIENTS

- ¼ cup egg substitute
- 1 muffin
- 1 turkey sausage patty
- 1 tablespoon cheddar cheese

DIRECTIONS

1. In a skillet pour egg and cook on low heat
2. Place turkey sausage patty in a pan and cook for 4-5 minutes per side
3. On a toasted muffin place the cooked egg, top with a sausage patty and cheddar cheese
4. Serve when ready

STRAWBERRY MUFFINS

Serves: **8-12**

Prep Time: **10** Minutes

Cook Time: **20** Minutes

Total Time: **30** Minutes

INGREDIENTS

- 2 eggs
- 1 tablespoon olive oil
- 1 cup milk
- 2 cups whole wheat flour
- 1 tsp baking soda
- ¼ tsp baking soda
- 1 tsp cinnamon
- 1 cup strawberries

DIRECTIONS

1. In a bowl combine all wet ingredients
2. In another bowl combine all dry ingredients
3. Combine wet and dry ingredients together
4. Pour mixture into 8-12 prepared muffin cups, fill 2/3 of the cups
5. Bake for 18-20 minutes at 375 F
6. When ready remove from the oven and serve

Serves: **2**
Prep Time: **10** Minutes

Cook Time: **20** Minutes

Total Time: **30** Minutes

INGREDIENTS

- ½ lb. butternut
- 1 tablespoon olive oil
- ½ red onion
- 2 eggs
- ¼ tsp salt
- 2 oz. cheddar cheese
- 1 garlic clove
- ¼ tsp dill

DIRECTIONS

1. In a bowl whisk eggs with salt and cheese
2. In a frying pan heat olive oil and pour egg mixture
3. Add remaining ingredients and mix well
4. Serve when ready

CORIANDER FRITATTA

Serves: *2*
Prep Time: *10* Minutes

Cook Time: *20* Minutes

Total Time: *30* Minutes

INGREDIENTS

- ½ lb. spinach
- 1 tablespoon olive oil
- ½ red onion
- 2 eggs
- ¼ tsp salt
- 2 oz. cheddar cheese
- 1 garlic clove
- ¼ tsp dill
- 1 tablespoon coriander

DIRECTIONS

1. In a bowl whisk eggs with salt and cheese
2. In a frying pan heat olive oil and pour egg mixture
3. Add remaining ingredients and mix well
4. Serve when ready

DILL FRITATTA

Serves: **2**
Prep Time: **10**   Minutes

Cook Time: **20**   Minutes

Total Time: **30**   Minutes

INGREDIENTS

- 1 tablespoon olive oil
- ½ red onion
- ¼ tsp salt
- 2 eggs
- 2 oz. cheddar cheese
- 1 garlic clove
- 1 tsp dill

DIRECTIONS

1. In a bowl whisk eggs with salt and cheese
2. In a frying pan heat olive oil and pour egg mixture
3. Add remaining ingredients and mix well
4. Serve when ready

PROSCIUTTO FRITATTA

Serves: **2**
Prep Time: **10** Minutes

Cook Time: **20** Minutes

Total Time: **30** Minutes

INGREDIENTS

- 8-10 slices prosciutto
- 1 tablespoon olive oil
- ½ red onion
- ¼ tsp salt
- 2 eggs
- 2 oz. parmesan cheese
- 1 garlic clove
- ¼ tsp dill

DIRECTIONS

1. In a bowl whisk eggs with salt and parmesan cheese
2. In a frying pan heat olive oil and pour egg mixture
3. Add remaining ingredients and mix well
4. When prosciutto and eggs are cooked remove from heat and serve

PEA FRITATTA

Serves: **2**
Prep Time: **10**   Minutes

Cook Time: **20**   Minutes

Total Time: **30**   Minutes

INGREDIENTS

- ½ lb. pea
- 1 tablespoon olive oil
- ½ red onion
- ¼ tsp salt
- 2 oz. cheddar cheese
- 1 garlic clove
- 2 eggs
- ¼ tsp dill

DIRECTIONS

1. In a bowl whisk eggs with salt and cheese
2. In a frying pan heat olive oil and pour egg mixture
3. Add remaining ingredients and mix well
4. Serve when ready

DESSERTS

BREAKFAST COOKIES

Serves: **8-12**
Prep Time: **5**   Minutes

Cook Time: **15**   Minutes

Total Time: **20**   Minutes

INGREDIENTS

- 1 cup rolled oats
- ¼ cup applesauce
- ½ tsp vanilla extract
- 3 tablespoons chocolate chips
- 2 tablespoons dried fruits
- 1 tsp cinnamon

DIRECTIONS

1. Preheat the oven to 325 F
2. In a bowl combine all ingredients together and mix well
3. Scoop cookies using an ice cream scoop
4. Place cookies onto a prepared baking sheet
5. Place in the oven for 12-15 minutes or until the cookies are done
6. When ready remove from the oven and serve

PISTACHIOS ICE-CREAM

Serves: *6-8*

Prep Time: *15*   Minutes

Cook Time: *15*   Minutes

Total Time: *30*   Minutes

INGREDIENTS

- 4 egg yolks
- 1 cup heavy cream
- 1 cup milk
- 1 cup sugar
- 1 vanilla bean
- 1 tsp almond extract
- 1 cup cherries
- ½ cup pistachios

DIRECTIONS

1. In a saucepan whisk together all ingredients
2. Mix until bubbly
3. Strain into a bowl and cool
4. Whisk in favorite fruits and mix well
5. Cover and refrigerate for 2-3 hours
6. Pour mixture in the ice-cream maker and follow manufacturer instructions

VANILLA ICE-CREAM

Serves: **6-8**

Prep Time: **15**   Minutes
Cook Time: **15**   Minutes
Total Time: **30**   Minutes

INGREDIENTS

- 1 cup milk
- 1 tablespoon cornstarch
- 1 oz. cream cheese
- 1 cup heavy cream
- 1 cup brown sugar
- 1 tablespoon corn syrup
- 1 vanilla bean

DIRECTIONS

1. In a saucepan whisk together all ingredients
2. Mix until bubbly
3. Strain into a bowl and cool
4. Whisk in favorite fruits and mix well
5. Cover and refrigerate for 2-3 hours
6. Pour mixture in the ice-cream maker and follow manufacturer instructions
7. Serve when ready

COFFE ICE-CREAM

Serves: **6-8**

Prep Time: **15**   Minutes
Cook Time: **15**   Minutes
Total Time: **30**   Minutes

INGREDIENTS

- 4 egg yolks
- 1 cup black coffee
- 2 cups heavy cream
- 1 cup half-and-half
- 1 cup brown sugar
- 1 tsp vanilla extract

DIRECTIONS

1. In a saucepan whisk together all ingredients
2. Mix until bubbly
3. Strain into a bowl and cool
4. Whisk in favorite fruits and mix well
5. Cover and refrigerate for 2-3 hours
6. Pour mixture in the ice-cream maker and follow manufacturer instructions
7. Serve when ready

STRAWBERRY ICE-CREAM

Serves: *6-8*

Prep Time: *15*   Minutes

Cook Time: *15*   Minutes

Total Time: *30*   Minutes

INGREDIENTS

- 1 lb. strawberries
- ½ cup sugar
- 1 tablespoon vanilla extract
- 1 cup heavy cram
- 1-pint vanilla

DIRECTIONS

1. In a saucepan whisk together all ingredients
2. Mix until bubbly
3. Strain into a bowl and cool
4. Whisk in favorite fruits and mix well
5. Cover and refrigerate for 2-3 hours
6. Pour mixture in the ice-cream maker and follow manufacturer instructions
7. Serve when ready

SMOOTHIES AND DRINKS

WATERMELON SMOOTHIE

Serves: **1**

Prep Time: **5**   Minutes

Cook Time: **5**   Minutes

Total Time: **10**   Minutes

INGREDIENTS

- 2 cups watermelon
- 1 cup almond milk
- 1 cup vanilla yogurt
- 2 tablespoons maple syrup
- 1 cup ice

DIRECTIONS

1. In a blender place all ingredients and blend until smooth
2. Pour smoothie in a glass and serve

COCONUT SMOOTHIE

Serves: **1**
Prep Time: **5**   Minutes

Cook Time: **5**   Minutes

Total Time: **10**   Minutes

INGREDIENTS

- 2 cup pineapple
- ¼ cup coconut milk
- 1 cup pineapple juice
- 2 tablespoons coconut flakes
- ½ cup yogurt
- 1 tablespoon honey

DIRECTIONS

1. In a blender place all ingredients and blend until smooth
2. Pour smoothie in a glass and serve

Serves: *1*

Prep Time: *5*   Minutes

Cook Time: *5*   Minutes

Total Time: *10*   Minutes

INGREDIENTS

- 1 cup raspberries
- 1 cup strawberries
- 1 banana
- 1 cup almond milk
- 1 tablespoon honey
- 1 cup ice

DIRECTIONS

1. In a blender place all ingredients and blend until smooth
2. Pour smoothie in a glass and serve

Serves: *1*
Prep Time: *5*   Minutes

Cook Time: *5*   Minutes

Total Time: *10*   Minutes

INGREDIENTS

- 1 apple
- 1 pear
- 1 cup coconut water
- 1 tablespoon honey

DIRECTIONS

1. In a blender place all ingredients and blend until smooth
2. Pour smoothie in a glass and serve

Serves: *1*
Prep Time: 5   Minutes

Cook Time: 5   Minutes

Total Time: *10* Minutes

INGREDIENTS

- 1 avocado
- 1 cup spinach
- 1 banana
- ½ cup cauliflower
- 2 dates
- 1 cup almond milk

DIRECTIONS

1. In a blender place all ingredients and blend until smooth
2. Pour smoothie in a glass and serve

CLASSIC STRAWBERRY SMOOTHIE

Serves: *1*
Prep Time: 5   Minutes

Cook Time: 5   Minutes

Total Time: *10*   Minutes

INGREDIENTS

- 1 cup strawberries
- 1 banana
- 1 cup Greek Yogurt
- 1 cup orange juice

DIRECTIONS

1. In a blender place all ingredients and blend until smooth
2. Pour smoothie in a glass and serve

Serves: *1*
Prep Time: 5   Minutes

Cook Time: 5   Minutes

Total Time: *10* Minutes

INGREDIENTS

- 2 cups banana
- 1 tablespoon flax seeds
- 1 cup almond milk
- 1 tsp vanilla extract
- 2 tablespoon peanut butter

DIRECTIONS

1. In a blender place all ingredients and blend until smooth
2. Pour smoothie in a glass and serve

SPINACH SMOOTHIE

Serves: *1*

Prep Time: *5* Minutes

Cook Time: *5* Minutes

Total Time: *10* Minutes

INGREDIENTS

- 2 cups banana
- 2 cups strawberries
- 2 cups spinach
- 2 chia seeds

DIRECTIONS

1. In a blender place all ingredients and blend until smooth
2. Pour smoothie in a glass and serve

PROTEIN SMOOTHIE

Serves: *1*

Prep Time: 5   Minutes

Cook Time: 5   Minutes

Total Time: *10*   Minutes

INGREDIENTS

- 1 cup berries
- 1 tablespoon chia seeds
- ½ cup protein powder
- 1 cup almond milk

DIRECTIONS

1. In a blender place all ingredients and blend until smooth
2. Pour smoothie in a glass and serve

Serves: *1*
Prep Time: *5*   Minutes

Cook Time: *5*   Minutes

Total Time: *10*   Minutes

INGREDIENTS

- ½ cup oatmeal
- ½ cup protein powder
- 1 tablespoon peanut butter
- 1 cup coconut milk
- 1 banana

DIRECTIONS

1. In a blender place all ingredients and blend until smooth
2. Pour smoothie in a glass and serve

SECOND COOKBOOK

ROASTED CHERRY & RICOTTA TARTINE

Serves: *2*

Prep Time: *20*   Minutes

Cook Time: *30*   Minutes

Total Time: *50*   Minutes

INGREDIENTS

- 2 cups cherries
- 1 tablespoon honey
- 1 tsp lemon zest
- 1 tablespoon lemon juice
- 1 tsp olive oil
- salt
- 4 slices bread
- 1 cup part-skim ricotta cheese
- 1 tsp thyme
- ½ cup almonds

DIRECTIONS

1. Preheat the oven to 375 F
2. In a bowl toss with lemon juice, oil, honey and roast them for about 12-15 minutes

3. Toast bread and top with lemon zest, ricotta cheese, cherries, thyme, almonds, and salt

4. Drizzle with honey and serve

MORNING MANGO BOWL

Serves: **4**

Prep Time: **10**   Minutes

Cook Time: **10**   Minutes

Total Time: **20**   Minutes

INGREDIENTS

- ½ cup mango
- ¼ cup Greek Yogurt
- ½ cup banana
- ½ cup unsweetened almond milk
- 4 tablespoons almonds
- ½ tsp allspice
- ½ cup raspberries
- ¼ tsp honey

DIRECTIONS

1. In a blender add all ingredients and blend until smooth
2. Pour the mango yogurt into a bowl and serve with raspberries and almonds

Serves: **4**

Prep Time: **10**   Minutes

Cook Time: **30**   Minutes

Total Time: **40**   Minutes

INGREDIENTS

- 1 oz. ham
- 1 oz. turkey
- 1 oz. Swiss cheese
- 1 egg
- 3 leaves romaine lettuce
- ½ cup yellow bell pepper
- ½ cup red onion
- ½ cup cucumber
- 1 tomato
- 1 carrot
- 1 tablespoon salad dressing
- 2 large tomato wraps

DIRECTIONS

1. Roll ham, turkey and Swiss cheese and cut into thin strips, toss with vegetables and roll your tortilla
2. Place a tablespoon of dressing on your tortilla

CHOCOLATE OAT BARS

Serves: **4**

Prep Time: **10**   Minutes

Cook Time: **30**   Minutes

Total Time: **40**   Minutes

INGREDIENTS

- 1 egg
- ¼ cup yogurt
- ¼ cup brown sugar
- 1 cup quick oats
- 1 tablespoon flaxseed
- ½ cup chocolate chips

DIRECTIONS

1. In a bowl whisk yogurt, egg, and sugar
2. In a blender add oats, flaxseed, chocolate chips, egg mixture and blend until smooth
3. Spread mixture in a pan and bake at 325 F for 25 min
4. Remove, cut into bars and serve

Serves: **4**

Prep Time: **10** Minutes

Cook Time: **30** Minutes

Total Time: **40** Minutes

INGREDIENTS

- 2 cups water
- 1 cup brown rice
- 1 cup milk
- 1 cup Splenda
- 1 cup crystallized ginger

DIRECTIONS

1. In a saucepan bring water and rice to a boil, reduce heat and cook for 25-30 minutes
2. Stir in Splenda while rice is cooking
3. Add milk, ginger and spend and cook until milk is absorbed
4. Remove from heat garnish with orange slices and serve

Serves: *3*
Prep Time: *10*   Minutes

Cook Time: *35*   Minutes

Total Time: *45*   Minutes

INGREDIENTS

- 2 egg whites
- ½ cup Splenda
- ½ tsp vanilla
- 1 tablespoon lemon curd

DIRECTIONS

1. In a bowl beat egg whites, add Splenda and continue to mix
2. Stir in vanilla and mix well
3. Drop mixture using a pipe onto a baking sheet making around 10-12 portions
4. Bake at 275 F for 25-30 minutes
5. Remove and serve

LEMONADE

Serves: *2*
Prep Time: *10*   Minutes

Cook Time: *10*   Minutes

Total Time: *20*   Minutes

INGREDIENTS

- 1 lemon
- 1 packet sweet
- 1 cup water
- 1 cup ice cubes

DIRECTIONS

1. Cut lemon in half and squeeze the juice into a glass
2. Add sweetener, water, and ice cubes
3. Mix well, garnish with a strawberry and serve

MORNING PIE

Serves: **8**

Prep Time: **10**   Minutes

Cook Time: **35**   Minutes

Total Time: **45**   Minutes

INGREDIENTS

- **1 15 oz. can pumpkin**
- **½ cup egg substitute**
- **¾ cup sugar**
- **1 tsp cinnamon**
- **¼ tsp ground ginger**
- **½ tsp nutmeg**
- **½ tsp cloves**
- **1 12 oz. can evaporated skim milk**

CRUST

- **1 cup flour**
- **2 tablespoons water**
- **½ cup shortening**

DIRECTIONS

1. **Preheat the oven to 400 F**

2. Place shortening, water, and flour into a bowl and mix well and form a ball

3. Let it stand for 20-30 minutes and then roll crust in a pan

4. In a whisk together pumpkin, sugar, egg substitute, evaporated milk and mix well

5. Pour mixture into pie shell and bake for 35 minutes

6. Remove and serve

FRUIT TARTS

Serves: **2**
Prep Time: **10** Minutes

Cook Time: **20** Minutes

Total Time: **30** Minutes

INGREDIENTS

- 1 tart apple
- 1 tablespoon Splenda
- ½ tsp cinnamon
- 10 wonton wrappers

DIRECTIONS

1. Preheat the oven to 325 F
2. Grate the apples and sprinkle with cinnamon and Splenda
3. Fill a muffin pan with grated apple and bake for 10-12 minutes, remove and serve

MORNING ICE TEA

Serves: **1**

Prep Time: **10** Minutes

Cook Time: **10** Minutes

Total Time: **20** Minutes

INGREDIENTS

- 3 cups cold water
- 2 peaches tea bags
- 1 cup ice cubes

DIRECTIONS

1. Pour water, ice cubes and tea bags in a glass
2. After 2-3 minutes remove tea bags and serve

Serves: *4*
Prep Time: *10*   Minutes

Cook Time: *30*   Minutes

Total Time: *40*   Minutes

INGREDIENTS

- 1 kiwi
- ½ cup strawberries
- ¾ seltzer
- 1 cup ice cubes

DIRECTIONS

1. In a bowl mash kiwi and strawberries
2. Pour juice, ice, and top with seltzer
3. Mix well and serve

Serves: **4**

Prep Time: **10** Minutes

Cook Time: **10** Minutes

Total Time: **20** Minutes

INGREDIENTS

- ½ cup ketchup
- ½ cup oil
- ½ cup white vinegar
- 1 tsp lemon juice
- 4 bread slices

DIRECTIONS

1. In a bowl stir all ingredients until well combined
2. Dip the bread into the mixture
3. Fry bread for 1-2 minutes per side
4. Remove and serve

Serves: *4*
Prep Time: *10*   Minutes

Cook Time: *30*   Minutes

Total Time: *40*   Minutes

INGREDIENTS

- 1 cup dark rum
- 1 tsp lemon rind
- ¾ cup artificial sweetener
- 1 cup walnuts
- 1 cup pecans
- 3 cups cranberries

DIRECTIONS

1. In a saucepan add Splenda, rum and bring to a boil
2. Add cranberries, lemon zest and simmer on low heat for 12-15 minutes
3. Add nuts cook for 2-3 minutes, remove and serve

Serves:	**2**
Prep Time:	**10** Minutes
Cook Time:	**10** Minutes
Total Time:	**20** Minutes

INGREDIENTS

- 2 bananas
- 1 cup strawberries
- 1 cup blackberries
- 1 cup chopped pineapple
- 1 cup coconut milk
- 1 tablespoon whole grain granola
- ¼ ounce roasted coconut chips

DIRECTIONS

1. Slice the bananas and place them into a bowl
2. Divide the strawberries, blackberries, and pineapple and place it in the bottom of the bowl
3. Top with yogurt and divide the granola and coconut chips between the bananas

CHAI-SPICED PEAR OATMEAL

Serves: **2**

Prep Time: **10** Minutes

Cook Time: **30** Minutes

Total Time: **40** Minutes

INGREDIENTS

- 1 cup oats
- ½ tsp ground cinnamon
- 1 tsp maple syrup
- 1 tablespoon walnut halves
- 2 tsp coconut oil
- 1 Anjou pear spiralized
- 1 cup almond milk
- ½ tsp vanilla extract

DIRECTIONS

1. In a saucepan boil water and add oats for another 10 minutes
2. In a skillet heat coconut oil over medium heat and add almond milk, pear noodles, cinnamon, maple syrup, and vanilla extract
3. Stir to simmer for about 10-15 minutes
4. In another skillet place walnuts and cook for 5-6 minutes, remove from the pan when ready

5. Place the oatmeal in a bowl and top with pear mixture and toasted walnuts

Serves: **4**

Prep Time: **10**   Minutes

Cook Time: **10**   Minutes

Total Time: **20**   Minutes

INGREDIENTS

- ½ cup rice flour
- 1 tsp baking soda
- 1 banana
- ½ tsp salt
- 2 tablespoons oil
- ½ cup milk
- 1 tsp cider vinegar
- 1 egg
- ½ cup quinoa flakes
- 1 tablespoon honey

DIRECTIONS

1. In a bowl mix all dry ingredients
2. Separate egg yolk from egg white and beat egg whites
3. Mix egg yolk with milk, honey, wet fruit and add dry ingredients to mixture
4. Add cider vinegar and mix gently

5. Pour mixture into waffle iron
6. When ready remove and serve

Serves: **12**

Prep Time: **10** Minutes

Cook Time: **15** Minutes

Total Time: **25** Minutes

INGREDIENTS

- 2 cups flour
- 1 tsp xantham gum
- ½ tsp salt
- 4 tablespoons margarine
- 1 tablespoon baking powder
- 1 tsp sugar

DIRECTIONS

1. Preheat oven to 425 F
2. Toss together all ingredients, gather into a ball
3. Form small biscuits and bake for 12-15 minutes
4. Remove and serve

MUSHROOM OMELETTE

Serves: **1**

Prep Time: **5** Minutes

Cook Time: **10** Minutes

Total Time: **15** Minutes

INGREDIENTS

- 2 eggs
- ¼ tsp salt
- ¼ tsp black pepper
- 1 tablespoon olive oil
- ¼ cup cheese
- ¼ tsp basil
- 1 cup mushrooms

DIRECTIONS

1. In a bowl combine all ingredients together and mix well
2. In a skillet heat olive oil and pour the egg mixture
3. Cook for 1-2 minutes per side
4. When ready remove omelette from the skillet and serve

CABBAGE OMELETTE

Serves: *1*
Prep Time: *5*   Minutes

Cook Time: *10*   Minutes

Total Time: *15*   Minutes

INGREDIENTS

- 2 eggs
- 1 cup cabbage
- 1 cup cheese
- 1 tsp salt

DIRECTIONS

1. In a bowl combine all ingredients together and mix well
2. In a skillet heat olive oil and pour the egg mixture
3. Cook for 1-2 minutes per side
4. When ready remove omelette from the skillet and serve

TOASTED OATMEAL WITH SPICES

Serves: *2*
Prep Time: *5*   Minutes

Cook Time: *10*   Minutes

Total Time: *15*   Minutes

INGREDIENTS

- 1 cup gluten- free oats
- 2 cup water
- 1 cup unsweetened coconut
- 1 tsp vanilla extract
- ¼ tsp cinnamon
- ¼ tsp nutmeg
- 1 tablespoon coconut oil
- 1 apple
- 1 tablespoon maple syrup

DIRECTIONS

1. In a saucepan heat coconut oil, add oats and coconut flakes and toast for 2-3 minutes
2. Add water, milk, vanilla, nutmeg and stir
3. Serve with apple slices, cinnamon and maple syrup

PANCAKES

BANANA PANCAKES

Serves: **4**

Prep Time: **10**   Minutes

Cook Time: **20**   Minutes

Total Time: **30**   Minutes

INGREDIENTS

- 1 cup whole wheat flour
- ¼ tsp baking soda
- ¼ tsp baking powder
- 1 cup mashed banana
- 2 eggs
- 1 cup milk

DIRECTIONS

1. In a bowl combine all ingredients together and mix well
2. In a skillet heat olive oil
3. Pour ¼ of the batter and cook each pancake for 1-2 minutes per side
4. When ready remove from heat and serve

Serves: **6**

Prep Time: **5**   Minutes

Cook Time: **10** Minutes

Total Time: **15** Minutes

INGREDIENTS

- 1 apple
- 1 cup almond flour
- ¼ tsp baking powder
- ¼ tsp salt
- 2 eggs
- 1 tablespoon olive oil

DIRECTIONS

1. In a bowl combine all ingredients together
2. In a skillet heat olive oil and pour 1/6 batter
3. Cook for 1-2 minutes per side
4. When ready remove from the skillet and serve

SMOOTHIES

BANANA SMOOTHIE

Serves: *1*
Prep Time: 5   Minutes

Cook Time: 5   Minutes

Total Time: *10*   Minutes

INGREDIENTS

- ¼ cup strawberries
- ½ banana
- 1 orange
- 1 cup ice

DIRECTIONS

1. In a blender place all ingredients and blend until smooth
2. Pour smoothie in a glass and serve

Serves:	*1*	
Prep Time:	5	Minutes
Cook Time:	5	Minutes
Total Time:	*10*	Minutes

INGREDIENTS

- 1 banana
- 1 handful of blueberries
- 1 tablespoon coconut oil
- 1 tablespoon hemp seeds
- 1 tablespoon chia seeds
- pinch of cinnamon

DIRECTIONS

1. In a blender place all ingredients and blend until smooth
2. Pour smoothie in a glass and serve

Serves: *1*

Prep Time: 5   Minutes

Cook Time: 5   Minutes

Total Time: *10*   Minutes

INGREDIENTS

- ¼ cucumber
- 1 cup blueberries
- 6 oz. coconut water
- 1 tablespoon chia seeds
- 1 tablespoon honey
- ice cubes

DIRECTIONS

1. In a blender place all ingredients and blend until smooth
2. Pour smoothie in a glass and serve

Serves: *1*
Prep Time: 5   Minutes

Cook Time: 5   Minutes

Total Time: *10*   Minutes

INGREDIENTS

- 1 cup mixed berries
- ½ cup cranberry juice
- ½ avocado
- 1 cup coconut water
- 1 tablespoon chia seeds
- 1 tsp ginger

DIRECTIONS

1. In a blender place all ingredients and blend until smooth
2. Pour smoothie in a glass and serve

PUMPKIN SMOOTHIE

Serves: **1**

Prep Time: **5** Minutes

Cook Time: **5** Minutes

Total Time: **10** Minutes

INGREDIENTS

- ½ cup pumpkin
- ½ cup coconut milk
- 1 tablespoon chia seeds
- ½ cup coconut water
- 1 tsp honey
- 1 tsp cinnamon
- ¼ tsp nutmeg
- ¼ tsp pumpkin pie spice

DIRECTIONS

1. In a blender place all ingredients and blend until smooth
2. Pour smoothie in a glass and serve

CINNAMON-BLACKBERRY SMOOTHIE

Serves: *1*
Prep Time: *5*   Minutes

Cook Time: *5*   Minutes

Total Time: *10* Minutes

INGREDIENTS

- 1 cup blackberries
- 1 cup coconut water
- 1 tablespoon chia seeds
- ¼ tsp cinnamon
- 1 handful spinach
- 1 tablespoon honey

DIRECTIONS

1. In a blender place all ingredients and blend until smooth
2. Pour smoothie in a glass and serve

Serves: *1*
Prep Time: 5   Minutes

Cook Time: 5   Minutes

Total Time: *10*   Minutes

INGREDIENTS

- 1 cup Kale
- 1 apple
- 1 lemon
- 1-inch ginger
- 1 cup water

DIRECTIONS

1. In a blender place all ingredients and blend until smooth
2. Pour smoothie in a glass and serve

Serves: **1**
Prep Time: **5**   Minutes

Cook Time: **5**   Minutes

Total Time: **10**   Minutes

INGREDIENTS

- 1 cup coconut water
- 1 handful kale
- 1 handful spinach
- 4 stalks celery
- 1 apple
- juice of 1 lemon
- ¼ bunch parsley

DIRECTIONS

1. In a blender place all ingredients and blend until smooth
2. Pour smoothie in a glass and serve

COOKIES

BANANA COOKIES

Serves: *8*
Prep Time: *10*   Minutes

Cook Time: *10*   Minutes

Total Time: *20*   Minutes

INGREDIENTS

- 2 medjool dates
- ¼ cup butter
- ¼ cup desiccated coconut
- ¼ cup walnuts
- 2 tablespoons banana flour
- Stevia extract
- ¼ tsp cinnamon

DIRECTIONS

1. In a blender add all ingredients and blend until smooth
2. Remove from the blender and roll into balls
3. Sprinkle with coconut and refrigerate
4. When ready remove from the fridge and serve

Serves: **8-12**
Prep Time: **5**   Minutes

Cook Time: **15**   Minutes

Total Time: **20**   Minutes

INGREDIENTS

- 1 cup rolled oats
- ¼ cup applesauce
- ½ tsp vanilla extract
- 3 tablespoons chocolate chips
- 2 tablespoons dried fruits
- 1 tsp cinnamon

DIRECTIONS

1. Preheat the oven to 325 F
2. In a bowl combine all ingredients together and mix well
3. Scoop cookies using an ice cream scoop
4. Place cookies onto a prepared baking sheet
5. Place in the oven for 12-15 minutes or until the cookies are done
6. When ready remove from the oven and serve

BROWNIE COOKIES

Serves: **4**

Prep Time: **10** Minutes

Cook Time: **30** Minutes

Total Time: **40** Minutes

INGREDIENTS

- 2 oz. unsweetened chocolate
- 1 stick butter
- 1 cup Splenda
- 1 egg
- ¼ tsp vanilla
- ¾ cup whole-wheat flour
- ½ tsp baking soda
- ¼ cup chocolate chips
- ¼ cup walnuts

DIRECTIONS

1. Preheat the oven to 325 F
2. Microwave chocolate for 30 seconds
3. In another bowl mix Splenda, butter, vanilla, and the egg
4. Stir in melted chocolate, baking soda, flour, chocolate chips, and nuts

5. Drop teaspoons of batter onto the baking sheet and bake for 10-12 minutes

6. Remove and serve

MUFFINS

SIMPLE MUFFINS

Serves: **8-12**

Prep Time: **10** Minutes

Cook Time: **20** Minutes

Total Time: **30** Minutes

INGREDIENTS

- 2 eggs
- 1 tablespoon olive oil
- 1 cup milk
- 2 cups whole wheat flour
- 1 tsp baking soda
- ¼ tsp baking soda
- 1 cup pumpkin puree
- 1 tsp cinnamon
- ¼ cup molasses

DIRECTIONS

1. In a bowl combine all dry ingredients
2. In another bowl combine all dry ingredients
3. Combine wet and dry ingredients together
4. Pour mixture into 8-12 prepared muffin cups, fill 2/3 of the cups

5. Bake for 18-20 minutes at 375 F
6. When ready remove from the oven and serve

ZUCCHINI MUFFINS

Serves: *8*
Prep Time: *10*   Minutes

Cook Time: *30*   Minutes

Total Time: *40*   Minutes

INGREDIENTS

- 2 cups almond flour
- 1 tsp baking powder
- 1 zucchini
- 1 tablespoon flaxseed
- 1 tablespoon honey
- 1 tsp oregano

DIRECTIONS

1. In a bowl combine water and flaxseed meal
2. Add all dry and wet ingredients, mix well
3. Pour mixture into 8-10 muffin cups
4. Bake for 20-25 minutes at 400 F
5. When ready remove and serve

CHOCOLATE MUFFINS

Serves: *8*

Prep Time: *10*   Minutes

Cook Time: *30*   Minutes

Total Time: *40*   Minutes

INGREDIENTS

- 2 cups rice flour
- ¼ cup cornmeal
- 1 tablespoon baking powder
- ¼ tsp salt
- ¼ tsp nutmeg
- ¼ tsp chili powder
- ¼ cup cocoa powder
- 1 tablespoon flaxseed meal
- ¼ cup honey
- ¼ cup almond milk
- ¼ cup coconut oil
- ¼ cup olive oil

DIRECTIONS

1. In a bowl combine water and flaxseed meal
2. Add all dry and wet ingredients, mix well

3. Pour mixture into 8-10 muffin cups
4. Bake for 20-25 minutes at 400 F
5. When ready remove and serve

Serves: *8*
Prep Time: *15*   Minutes

Cook Time: *35*   Minutes

Total Time: *50*   Minutes

INGREDIENTS

- 2 tablespoons flaxseed
- ¼ cup water
- 1 cup sweet potato
- 1 cup apple sauce
- ¼ cup ghee
- 1 tablespoon maple syrup
- 1 cup rice flour
- 1 tsp baking powder
- 2 tsp chai mix
- 1 tsp salt

DIRECTIONS

1. In a bowl combine water and flaxseed meal
2. Add all dry and wet ingredients, mix well
3. Pour mixture into 8-10 muffin cups
4. Bake for 20-25 minutes at 400 F, when ready remove and serve

COCONUT MUFFINS

Serves: **4**

Prep Time: **10**   Minutes

Cook Time: **30**   Minutes

Total Time: **40**   Minutes

INGREDIENTS

- 2 bananas
- 1 tablespoon olive oil
- ¼ tsp baking powder
- ¼ tsp salt
- ½ cup coconut flour
- 1 tablespoon coconut flakes

DIRECTIONS

1. In a bowl combine wet and dry ingredients together and mix well
2. Pour mixture into 8-10 muffin cups
3. Bake for 20-25 minutes at 400 F
4. When ready remove and serve

Serves: *8*

Prep Time: *10*   Minutes

Cook Time: *20*   Minutes

Total Time: *30*   Minutes

INGREDIENTS

- 1 cup oats
- 1 cup flour
- 1 tsp baking powder
- ½ tsp salt
- ¾ cup brown sugar
- 1 egg
- 1 cup skim milk
- 1/2 cup vegetable oil
- 1 carrot
- 1 cup raisins
- ¼ cup walnuts

DIRECTIONS

1. Preheat the oven to 375 F
2. In a bowl mix flour, oats, salt, baking powder, and sugar
3. In another bowl beat eggs and carrots, vegetable oil and milk

4. Stir wet ingredients into dry ingredients and mix well
5. Stir in walnuts raisins and divide batter into 8-10 muffin cups
6. Bake for 18-20 minutes, remove and serve

THIRD COOKBOOK

ZUCCHINI APPLE PANCAKES

Serves: **4**

Prep Time: **10** minutes

Cook Time: **10** minutes

Total Time: **20** minutes

INGREDIENTS

- 1 zucchini
- 2 tablespoons almond butter
- 2 eggs
- 1 tablespoon honey
- 2 tablespoons coconut oil
- 1 apple
- 1 cup almond flour
- ¼ tsp baking powder
- ¼ tsp sea salt

DIRECTIONS

1. Mix zucchini, honey, apples, thyme and almond butter in a bowl
2. In another bowl mix salt, baking powder and flour and beat the eggs
3. Mix all the ingredients from the bowl and heat coconut oil in a fry pan

4. Pour the mixture in the pan and cook for 1-2 minutes each side

Serves: **4**
Prep Time: **5**   Minutes

Cook Time: **10**   Minutes

Total Time: **15**   Minutes

INGREDIENTS

-   1 cup quinoa
-   1 cup goji
-   parsley as needed

DIRECTIONS

1. Soak the quinoa and goji grains for 5-6 minutes in water
2. Cook quinoa until soft for 10-15 minutes
3. Roast the cumin seeds in a hot pan and stir in goji berries and sprinkle with parsley

Serves: **2**
Prep Time: **10**   Minutes

Cook Time: **20**   Minutes

Total Time: **30**   Minutes

INGREDIENTS

- 2 cloves garlic
- 2 sausages
- ¼ onion
- ¼ cup carrot
- 2 cups mushrooms
- 1 tsp coconut oil
- ¼ tablespoon parsley
- 2 cups asparagus

DIRECTIONS

1. Sauté the garlic and onions in coconut oil and add the rest of the ingredients
2. Add the sausages and cook for 5-10 minutes, serve when ready

Serves: **3**

Prep Time: **10** Minutes

Cook Time: **10** Minutes

Total Time: **20** Minutes

INGREDIENTS

- 1 cauliflower heat
- 1 tablespoon salt
- 1 tablespoon pepper
- basil
- 1 tablespoon coconut oil
- 1 tablespoon parsley

DIRECTIONS

1. **Grate the cauliflower to rice-grain**
2. **In a pan melt coconut oil add basil and add cauliflower and cook for 5-10 minutes**
3. **Cook until ready, remove and serve**

HOMEMADE GRANOLA

Serves: *2*
Prep Time: *10* Minutes

Cook Time: *10* Minutes

Total Time: *20* Minutes

INGREDIENTS

- ¼ cup pumpkin seeds
- ¼ cup apricots
- 1 cup pecans
- ¼ cup almonds
- 1 cup coconut
- ½ cup coconut oil
- ½ cup honey
- 1 tsp cinnamon
- ¼ tsp nutmeg

DIRECTIONS

1. Preheat the oven to 325 F
2. Combine all the ingredients and toss well
3. Spread the mixture on a baking sheet (grease it with coconut oil) and bake for 10-15 minutes
4. When ready remove from oven and stir apricots
5. Let it cool and serve

FRENCH TOAST

Serves: **2**
Prep Time: **10**   Minutes

Cook Time: **10**   Minutes

Total Time: **20**   Minutes

INGREDIENTS

- 2 eggs
- zest of ½ orange
- butter
- 2 tablespoons milk
- 10 slices fruit bread

DIRECTIONS

1. In a bowl mix eggs, orange zest and eggs, beat the eggs before and mix everything together
2. Place a slice of bread into the mixture to soak
3. Place a pan over medium heat
4. Place the bread slices in the pan and cook for 1-2 minutes on each side
5. Remove and serve with maple syrup

COCONUT OMELETTE

Serves: *4*
Prep Time: *10* Minutes

Cook Time: *10* Minutes

Total Time: *20* Minutes

INGREDIENTS

- 2 eggs
- ½ tsp honey
- 1 tsp coconut oil

DIRECTIONS

1. In a bowl beat 2 eggs, add honey and stir
2. In a frying pan heat coconut oil over medium heat and pour the mixture
3. Cook on each side for 1-2 minutes
4. Remove and serve with salt or pepper

BANANA BREAKFAST CHEESECAKE

Serves: *1*

Prep Time: *10* Minutes

Cook Time: *10* Minutes

Total Time: *20* Minutes

INGREDIENTS

- 2 tsp chocolate chips
- vanilla extract
- 1 tsp almond butter
- 1 tsp honey
- 2 tablespoons oats
- 1 tablespoon cream cheese
- 1 banana

DIRECTIONS

1. In a bowl mix almond butter, oats and honey
2. Slice a banana and add it to the mixture
3. In the microwave add chocolate chips for 1 minute, add vanilla extract and cream cheese to the melted chocolate
4. Top the banana with chocolate mixture and serve

Serves: **4**
Prep Time: **10** Minutes

Cook Time: **30** Minutes

Total Time: **40** Minutes

INGREDIENTS

- 1 cup whole wheat flour
- ¼ tsp baking soda
- ¼ tsp baking powder
- 2 tablespoons goji berries
- 2 eggs
- 1 cup milk

DIRECTIONS

1. In a bowl combine all ingredients together and mix well
2. In a skillet heat olive oil
3. Pour ¼ of the batter and cook each pancake for 1-2 minutes per side
4. When ready remove from heat and serve

Serves: **4**
Prep Time: **10**   Minutes

Cook Time: **20**   Minutes

Total Time: **30**   Minutes

INGREDIENTS

- 1 cup whole wheat flour
- ¼ tsp baking soda
- ¼ tsp baking powder
- 1 cup mashed kiwi
- 2 eggs
- 1 cup milk

DIRECTIONS

1. In a bowl combine all ingredients together and mix well
2. In a skillet heat olive oil
3. Pour ¼ of the batter and cook each pancake for 1-2 minutes per side
4. When ready remove from heat and serve

MANGO PANCAKES

Serves: **4**

Prep Time: **10**   Minutes

Cook Time: **20**   Minutes

Total Time: **30**   Minutes

INGREDIENTS

- 1 cup whole wheat flour
- ¼ tsp baking soda
- ¼ tsp baking powder
- 1 cup mashed mango
- 2 eggs
- 1 cup milk

DIRECTIONS

1. In a bowl combine all ingredients together and mix well
2. In a skillet heat olive oil
3. Pour ¼ of the batter and cook each pancake for 1-2 minutes per side
4. When ready remove from heat and serve

Serves: **4**
Prep Time: **10** Minutes

Cook Time: **30** Minutes

Total Time: **40** Minutes

INGREDIENTS

- 1 cup whole wheat flour
- ¼ tsp baking soda
- ¼ tsp baking powder
- 2 eggs
- 1 cup milk

DIRECTIONS

1. In a bowl combine all ingredients together and mix well
2. In a skillet heat olive oil
3. Pour ¼ of the batter and cook each pancake for 1-2 minutes per side
4. When ready remove from heat and serve

GINGERBREAD MUFFINS

Serves: *8-12*

Prep Time: *10*   Minutes

Cook Time: *20*   Minutes

Total Time: *30*   Minutes

INGREDIENTS

- 2 eggs
- 1 tablespoon olive oil
- 1 cup milk
- 2 cups whole wheat flour
- 1 tsp baking soda
- ¼ tsp baking soda
- 1 tsp ginger
- 1 tsp cinnamon
- ¼ cup molasses

DIRECTIONS

1. In a bowl combine all wet ingredients
2. In another bowl combine all dry ingredients
3. Combine wet and dry ingredients together
4. Fold in ginger and mix well
5. Pour mixture into 8-12 prepared muffin cups, fill 2/3 of the cups

6. Bake for 18-20 minutes at 375 F
7. When ready remove from the oven and serve

PEAR MUFFINS

Serves: **8-12**
Prep Time: **10**   Minutes

Cook Time: **20**   Minutes

Total Time: **30**   Minutes

INGREDIENTS

- 2 eggs
- 1 tablespoon olive oil
- 1 cup milk
- 2 cups whole wheat flour
- 1 tsp baking soda
- ¼ tsp baking soda
- 1 tsp cinnamon
- 1 cup mashed pear

DIRECTIONS

1. In a bowl combine all wet ingredients
2. In another bowl combine all dry ingredients
3. Combine wet and dry ingredients together
4. Pour mixture into 8-12 prepared muffin cups, fill 2/3 of the cups
5. Bake for 18-20 minutes at 375 F
6. When ready remove from the oven and serve

POMELO MUFFINS

Serves: **8-12**
Prep Time: **10**   Minutes

Cook Time: **20**   Minutes

Total Time: **30**   Minutes

INGREDIENTS

- 2 eggs
- 1 tablespoon olive oil
- 1 cup milk
- 2 cups whole wheat flour
- 1 tsp baking soda
- ¼ tsp baking soda
- 1 tsp cinnamon
- 1 cup pomelo

DIRECTIONS

1. In a bowl combine all wet ingredients
2. In another bowl combine all dry ingredients
3. Combine wet and dry ingredients together
4. Pour mixture into 8-12 prepared muffin cups, fill 2/3 of the cups
5. Bake for 18-20 minutes at 375 F
6. When ready remove from the oven and serve

APPLE MUFFINS

Serves: *8-12*
Prep Time: *10*   Minutes

Cook Time: *20*   Minutes

Total Time: *30*   Minutes

INGREDIENTS

- 2 eggs
- 1 tablespoon olive oil
- 1 cup milk
- 2 cups whole wheat flour
- 1 tsp baking soda
- ¼ tsp baking soda
- 1 tsp cinnamon
- 1 cup apple

DIRECTIONS

1. In a bowl combine all wet ingredients
2. In another bowl combine all dry ingredients
3. Combine wet and dry ingredients together
4. Pour mixture into 8-12 prepared muffin cups, fill 2/3 of the cups
5. Bake for 18-20 minutes at 375 F
6. When ready remove from the oven and serve

CHOCOLATE MUFFINS

Serves: **8-12**
Prep Time: **10**   Minutes

Cook Time: **20**   Minutes

Total Time: **30**   Minutes

INGREDIENTS

- 2 eggs
- 1 tablespoon olive oil
- 1 cup milk
- 2 cups whole wheat flour
- 1 tsp baking soda
- ¼ tsp baking soda
- 1 tsp cinnamon
- 1 cup chocolate chips

DIRECTIONS

1. In a bowl combine all wet ingredients
2. In another bowl combine all dry ingredients
3. Combine wet and dry ingredients together
4. Fold in chocolate chips and mix well
5. Pour mixture into 8-12 prepared muffin cups, fill 2/3 of the cups
6. Bake for 18-20 minutes at 375 F, when ready remove and serve

SIMPLE MUFFINS

Serves: *8-12*
Prep Time: *10*   Minutes

Cook Time: *20*   Minutes

Total Time: *30*   Minutes

INGREDIENTS

- 2 eggs
- 1 tablespoon olive oil
- 1 cup milk
- 2 cups whole wheat flour
- 1 tsp baking soda
- ¼ tsp baking soda
- 1 tsp cinnamon

DIRECTIONS

1. In a bowl combine all wet ingredients
2. In another bowl combine all dry ingredients
3. Combine wet and dry ingredients together
4. Pour mixture into 8-12 prepared muffin cups, fill 2/3 of the cups
5. Bake for 18-20 minutes at 375 F
6. When ready remove from the oven and serve

SPINACH OMELETTE

Serves: *1*

Prep Time: *5*   Minutes

Cook Time: *10*   Minutes

Total Time: *15*   Minutes

INGREDIENTS

- 2 eggs
- ¼ tsp salt
- ¼ tsp black pepper
- 1 tablespoon olive oil
- ¼ cup cheese
- ¼ tsp basil
- 1 cup spinach

DIRECTIONS

1. In a bowl combine all ingredients together and mix well
2. In a skillet heat olive oil and pour the egg mixture
3. Cook for 1-2 minutes per side
4. When ready remove omelette from the skillet and serve

CUCUMBER OMELETTE

Serves: *1*

Prep Time: 5   Minutes

Cook Time: *10*   Minutes

Total Time: *15*   Minutes

INGREDIENTS

- 2 eggs
- ¼ tsp salt
- ¼ tsp black pepper
- 1 tablespoon olive oil
- ¼ cup cheese
- ¼ tsp basil
- ½ cup cucumber

DIRECTIONS

1. In a bowl combine all ingredients together and mix well
2. In a skillet heat olive oil and pour the egg mixture
3. Cook for 1-2 minutes per side
4. When ready remove omelette from the skillet and serve

BASIL OMELETTE

Serves: **1**

Prep Time: **5**   Minutes

Cook Time: **10**   Minutes

Total Time: **15**   Minutes

INGREDIENTS

- 2 eggs
- ¼ tsp salt
- ¼ tsp black pepper
- 1 tablespoon olive oil
- ¼ cup cheese
- ¼ tsp basil
- 1 cup red onion

DIRECTIONS

1. In a bowl combine all ingredients together and mix well
2. In a skillet heat olive oil and pour the egg mixture
3. Cook for 1-2 minutes per side
4. When ready remove omelette from the skillet and serve

CHEESE OMELETTE

Serves: *1*

Prep Time: *5*   Minutes

Cook Time: *10*   Minutes

Total Time: *15*   Minutes

INGREDIENTS

- 2 eggs
- ¼ tsp salt
- ¼ tsp black pepper
- 1 tablespoon olive oil
- ¼ cup cheese
- ¼ tsp basil
- 1 cup mushrooms

DIRECTIONS

1. In a bowl combine all ingredients together and mix well
2. In a skillet heat olive oil and pour the egg mixture
3. Cook for 1-2 minutes per side
4. When ready remove omelette from the skillet and serve

OLIVE OMELETTE

Serves: *1*
Prep Time: *5*   Minutes

Cook Time: *10*   Minutes

Total Time: *15*   Minutes

INGREDIENTS

- 2 eggs
- ¼ tsp salt
- ¼ tsp black pepper
- 1 tablespoon olive oil
- ¼ cup cheese
- ¼ cup Kalamata olives
- ¼ tsp basil
- 1 cup tomatoes

DIRECTIONS

1. In a bowl combine all ingredients together and mix well
2. In a skillet heat olive oil and pour the egg mixture
3. Cook for 1-2 minutes per side
4. When ready remove omelette from the skillet and serve

TART RECIPES

CARDAMOM TART

Serves: **6-8**

Prep Time: **25**   Minutes

Cook Time: **25**   Minutes

Total Time: **50**   Minutes

INGREDIENTS

- 4-5 pears
- 2 tablespoons lemon juice
- pastry sheets

CARDAMOM FILLING

- ½ lb. butter
- ½ lb. brown sugar
- ½ lb. almonds
- ¼ lb. flour
- 1 ¼ tsp cardamom
- 2 eggs

DIRECTIONS

1. Preheat oven to 400 F, unfold pastry sheets and place them on a baking sheet
2. Toss together all ingredients together and mix well

3. Spread mixture in a single layer on the pastry sheets
4. Before baking decorate with your desired fruits
5. Bake at 400 F for 22-25 minutes or until golden brown
6. When ready remove from the oven and serve

Serves: *6-8*
Prep Time: 25   Minutes

Cook Time: 25   Minutes

Total Time: *50*   Minutes

INGREDIENTS

- pastry sheets

FILLING

- 1 tsp lemon juice
- 3 oz. brown sugar
- 1 lb. apples
- 150 ml double cream
- 2 eggs

DIRECTIONS

1. Preheat oven to 400 F, unfold pastry sheets and place them on a baking sheet
2. Toss together all ingredients together and mix well
3. Spread mixture in a single layer on the pastry sheets
4. Before baking decorate with your desired fruits
5. Bake at 400 F for 22-25 minutes or until golden brown
6. When ready remove from the oven and serve

PIE RECIPES

PEACH PECAN PIE

Serves: *8-12*

Prep Time: *15*   Minutes

Cook Time: *35*   Minutes

Total Time: *50*   Minutes

INGREDIENTS

- 4-5 cups peaches
- 1 tablespoon preserves
- 1 cup sugar
- 4 small egg yolks
- ¼ cup flour
- 1 tsp vanilla extract

DIRECTIONS

1. Line a pie plate or pie form with pastry and cover the edges of the plate depending on your preference
2. In a bowl combine all pie ingredients together and mix well
3. Pour the mixture over the pastry
4. Bake at 400-425 F for 25-30 minutes or until golden brown
5. When ready remove from the oven and let it rest for 15 minutes

GRAPEFRUIT PIE

Serves: **8-12**

Prep Time: **15**   Minutes

Cook Time: **35**   Minutes

Total Time: **50**   Minutes

INGREDIENTS

- pastry sheets
- 2 cups grapefruit
- 1 cup brown sugar
- ¼ cup flour
- 5-6 egg yolks
- 5 oz. butter

DIRECTIONS

1. Line a pie plate or pie form with pastry and cover the edges of the plate depending on your preference
2. In a bowl combine all pie ingredients together and mix well
3. Pour the mixture over the pastry
4. Bake at 400-425 F for 25-30 minutes or until golden brown
5. When ready remove from the oven and let it rest for 15 minutes

BUTTERFINGER PIE

Serves: *8-12*

Prep Time: *15*   Minutes

Cook Time: *35*   Minutes

Total Time: *50*   Minutes

INGREDIENTS

- pastry sheets
- 1 package cream cheese
- 1 tsp vanilla extract
- ¼ cup peanut butter
- 1 cup powdered sugar (to decorate)
- 2 cups Butterfinger candy bars
- 8 oz whipped topping

DIRECTIONS

1. Line a pie plate or pie form with pastry and cover the edges of the plate depending on your preference
2. In a bowl combine all pie ingredients together and mix well
3. Pour the mixture over the pastry
4. Bake at 400-425 F for 25-30 minutes or until golden brown
5. When ready remove from the oven and let it rest for 15 minutes

BANANA MATCHA SMOOTHIE

Serves: *1*
Prep Time: *5*   Minutes

Cook Time: *5*   Minutes

Total Time: *10*   Minutes

INGREDIENTS

- 1 cup banana
- 1 tsp matcha powder
- 1 cup spinach
- 1 tsp flax seed
- 1 tsp vanilla extract
- 1 cup soy milk

DIRECTIONS

1. In a blender place all ingredients and blend until smooth
2. Pour smoothie in a glass and serve

PROTEIN SMOOTHIE

Serves:	*1*	
Prep Time:	5	Minutes
Cook Time:	5	Minutes
Total Time:	*10*	Minutes

INGREDIENTS

- 2 bananas
- 2 dates
- 1 cup kale
- 1 cup spinach
- 2 tablespoons cocoa powder
- 1 tsp vanilla extract
- 1 cup nut milk

DIRECTIONS

1. In a blender place all ingredients and blend until smooth
2. Pour smoothie in a glass and serve

Serves: *1*
Prep Time: 5   Minutes

Cook Time: 5   Minutes

Total Time: *10*   Minutes

INGREDIENTS

- 1 cup strawberries
- 1 banana
- 1 cup Greek Yogurt
- 1 cup soy milk
- 1 tsp vanilla extract
- 1 tsp chia seeds

DIRECTIONS

1. In a blender place all ingredients and blend until smooth
2. Pour smoothie in a glass and serve

POMEGRANATE SMOOTHIE

Serves: *1*

Prep Time: 5   Minutes

Cook Time: 5   Minutes

Total Time: *10*   Minutes

INGREDIENTS

- 1 cup strawberries
- 1 banana
- 1 cup Greek Yogurt
- 1 scoop protein powder
- 1 tsp hemp seeds
- ½ cup chocolate chips

DIRECTIONS

1. In a blender place all ingredients and blend until smooth
2. Pour smoothie in a glass and serve

APPLE SMOOTHIE

Serves: *1*
Prep Time: 5   Minutes

Cook Time: 5   Minutes

Total Time: *10*   Minutes

INGREDIENTS

- 1 apple
- 2 pears
- ½ cup rolled oats
- 1 tsp cinnamon
- 1 cup nut milk

DIRECTIONS

1. In a blender place all ingredients and blend until smooth
2. Pour smoothie in a glass and serve

SPINACH SMOOTHIE

Serves: *1*
Prep Time: 5   Minutes

Cook Time: 5   Minutes

Total Time: *10*   Minutes

INGREDIENTS

- 1 banana
- 1 cup vanilla yogurt
- 1 cup spinach
- 1 cup kale
- 1 cup orange juice

DIRECTIONS

1. In a blender place all ingredients and blend until smooth
2. Pour smoothie in a glass and serve

PEANUT BUTTER SMOOTHIE

Serves: **1**

Prep Time: **5**   Minutes

Cook Time: **5**   Minutes

Total Time: **10**   Minutes

INGREDIENTS

- 1 cup berries
- 2 tablespoons peanut butter
- ½ cup protein powder
- ½ cup oats
- 1 cup soy milk

DIRECTIONS

1. In a blender place all ingredients and blend until smooth
2. Pour smoothie in a glass and serve

PINEAPPLE SMOOTHIE

Serves: *1*
Prep Time: 5   Minutes

Cook Time: 5   Minutes

Total Time: *10*   Minutes

INGREDIENTS

- 1 cup pineapple
- 1 cup strawberries
- 1 cup Greek yogurt
- 1 cup soy milk
- 1 cup ice

DIRECTIONS

1. In a blender place all ingredients and blend until smooth
2. Pour smoothie in a glass and serve

Serves: *1*
Prep Time: 5   Minutes

Cook Time: 5   Minutes

Total Time: *10*   Minutes

INGREDIENTS

- 1 orange
- ½ cup orange juice
- ½ banana
- 1 tsp vanilla essence

DIRECTIONS

1. In a blender place all ingredients and blend until smooth
2. Pour smoothie in a glass and serve

RAISIN DATE SMOOTHIE

Serves: **1**

Prep Time: **5** Minutes

Cook Time: **5** Minutes

Total Time: **10** Minutes

INGREDIENTS

- ¼ cup raisins
- 2 Medjool dates
- 1 cup berries
- 1 cup almond milk
- 1 tsp chia seeds

DIRECTIONS

1. In a blender place all ingredients and blend until smooth
2. Pour smoothie in a glass and serve

PISTACHIOS ICE-CREAM

Serves: **6-8**

Prep Time: **15**   Minutes

Cook Time: **15**   Minutes

Total Time: **30**   Minutes

INGREDIENTS

- 4 egg yolks
- 1 cup heavy cream
- 1 cup milk
- 1 cup sugar
- 1 vanilla bean
- 1 tsp almond extract
- 1 cup cherries
- ½ cup pistachios

DIRECTIONS

1. In a saucepan whisk together all ingredients
2. Mix until bubbly
3. Strain into a bowl and cool
4. Whisk in favorite fruits and mix well
5. Cover and refrigerate for 2-3 hours

6. Pour mixture in the ice-cream maker and follow manufacturer instructions
7. Serve when ready

VANILLA ICE-CREAM

Serves: *6-8*

Prep Time: *15*   Minutes
Cook Time: *15*   Minutes
Total Time: *30*   Minutes

INGREDIENTS

- 1 cup milk
- 1 tablespoon cornstarch
- 1 oz. cream cheese
- 1 cup heavy cream
- 1 cup brown sugar
- 1 tablespoon corn syrup
- 1 vanilla bean

DIRECTIONS

1. In a saucepan whisk together all ingredients
2. Mix until bubbly
3. Strain into a bowl and cool
4. Whisk in favorite fruits and mix well
5. Cover and refrigerate for 2-3 hours
6. Pour mixture in the ice-cream maker and follow manufacturer instructions
7. Serve when ready

COFFE ICE-CREAM

Serves: **6-8**

Prep Time: **15**   Minutes
Cook Time: **15**   Minutes
Total Time: **30**   Minutes

INGREDIENTS

- 4 egg yolks
- 1 cup black coffee
- 2 cups heavy cream
- 1 cup half-and-half
- 1 cup brown sugar
- 1 tsp vanilla extract

DIRECTIONS

1. In a saucepan whisk together all ingredients
2. Mix until bubbly
3. Strain into a bowl and cool
4. Whisk in favorite fruits and mix well
5. Cover and refrigerate for 2-3 hours
6. Pour mixture in the ice-cream maker and follow manufacturer instructions
7. Serve when ready

FOURTH COOKBOOK

CHICKEN PIZZA

Serves: *2*

Prep Time: *10*   Minutes

Cook Time: *20*   Minutes

Total Time: *30*   Minutes

INGREDIENTS

- 1 ready-made pizza crust
- 1 tsp olive oil
- 1 cup onion
- 14 cup red pepper strips
- 1 cup chicken
- ¼ cup barbecue sauce
- 1 cup mozzarella cheese
- topping of any choice

DIRECTIONS

1. Preheat the oven to 425 F
2. In a frying pan add pepper strips, onion, chicken and cook on low heat
3. Cook until ready and remove from heat

4. Place crust on a cookie sheet and spread barbecue sauce, and the rest of ingredients on the crust

5. Top with mozzarella and bake for 12-15 minutes

6. Remove and serve

CIABATTA PIZZA

Serves: **2**
Prep Time: **10** Minutes

Cook Time: **20** Minutes

Total Time: **30** Minutes

INGREDIENTS

- 1 loaf ciabatta
- 1 cup tomato sauce
- 1 zucchini
- ½ cup mushrooms
- 1 cup mozzarella cheese
- 1 tablespoon basil

DIRECTIONS

1. Preheat the oven to 375 F
2. Cum ciabatta lengthwise and place on a cookie sheet
3. Spread sauce, zucchini, mushrooms on each one and top with mozzarella
4. Sprinkle basil, bake for 12-15 minutes, remove and serve

FIESTA SHRIMP

Serves: *2*

Prep Time: *10*   Minutes

Cook Time: *10*   Minutes

Total Time: *20*   Minutes

INGREDIENTS

- 3 oz. shrimp
- ½ cup zucchini
- ½ cup fiesta garden salsa
- ½ oz. Monterey Jack cheese
- cilantro
- 1 tortilla

DIRECTIONS

1. In a bowl add zucchini, shrimp and salsa
2. Microwave for 4-5 minutes, remove and add grated cheese
3. Sprinkle cilantro and pour mixture over tortilla
4. Serve when ready

GRILLED SALMON STEAKS

Serves: **2**
Prep Time: **10**   Minutes

Cook Time: **10**   Minutes

Total Time: **20**   Minutes

INGREDIENTS

- 2 salmon steaks
- 1 tablespoon dipping sauce
- 1 tsp cooking oil

DIRECTIONS

1. Preheat grill
2. Baste salmon steaks with sauce and cook for 5-6 minutes
3. Remove and serve

ORIENTAL GREENS

Serves: **2**
Prep Time: **10** Minutes

Cook Time: **10** Minutes

Total Time: **20** Minutes

INGREDIENTS

- ½ cup green beans
- ¼ cup snow peas
- 1 cup cauliflower florets
- 1 cup water chestnuts
- 2 radishes
- 2 scallions
- ½ cup red onion
- 1 tsp powdered ginger
- ½ cup rice wine vinegar

DIRECTIONS

1. In a bowl mix cauliflower floret, onions, chestnuts, radish, beans and snow peas
2. In another bowl mix rice wine vinegar, ginger, pour over vegetables and mix well
3. Mix well and serv

SHRIMP PIZZA

Serves: **2**

Prep Time: **10**   Minutes

Cook Time: **20**   Minutes

Total Time: **30**   Minutes

INGREDIENTS

- 13 oz. pizza dough
- 1 tablespoon cornmeal
- ¼ cup ricotta cheese
- 1 lb. shrimp
- 5 cloves garlic
- 1 cup mozzarella cheese
- 1 tablespoon dried basil

DIRECTIONS

1. Preheat the oven to 375 F
2. In a baking pan sprinkle cornmeal and add the pizza dough, bake for 6-8 minutes
3. Remove and cover pizza with mozzarella, ricotta, garlic and sprinkle with basil
4. Bake for 12-15 minutes, remove and serve

COLE SLAW

Serves: **2**

Prep Time: **10** Minutes

Cook Time: **10** Minutes

Total Time: **20** Minutes

INGREDIENTS

- 1/3 cup vinegar
- ¼ cup whipping cream
- 2 eggs
- ½ cup Splenda
- pinch of salt
- 1 tablespoon butter
- 1 lb. cabbage

DIRECTIONS

1. In a saucepan add vinegar, whipping cream, eggs, Splenda, and salt and cook for 10-12 minutes
2. Add butter, cabbage, toss to coat and mix well
3. Remove from heat add, walnuts and serve

DIJON VINAIGRETTE

Serves: **2**

Prep Time: **5**   Minutes

Cook Time: **5**   Minutes

Total Time: ***10***   Minutes

INGREDIENTS

- **2 tablespoons red wine vinegar**
- **1 tablespoon water**
- **1 tablespoon olive oil**
- **1 tsp Dijon mustard**
- **½ tsp garlic powder**

DIRECTIONS

1. **In a bowl mix all ingredients**
2. **Chill overnight and serve**

Serves: *3*
Prep Time: *10*   Minutes

Cook Time: *50*   Minutes

Total Time: *60*   Minutes

INGREDIENTS

- 2 eggs
- 2 cups cottage cheese
- 1 red onion
- 1 pinch of pepper

DIRECTIONS

1. In a bowl mix all ingredients and pour into a casserole dish
2. Bake at 325 for 50 minutes
3. Remove and serve

FRENCH DRESSING

Serves: **2**
Prep Time: **5**   Minutes

Cook Time: **5**   Minutes

Total Time: **10** Minutes

INGREDIENTS

- ½ cup ketchup
- ¼ cup oil
- ¼ cup white vinegar
- 1 tsp lemon juice
- dash of pepper

DIRECTIONS

1. **In a bowl mix all ingredients**
2. **Chill overnight and serve**

Serves: **4**
Prep Time: **10**   Minutes

Cook Time: **10**   Minutes

Total Time: **20**   Minutes

INGREDIENTS

- ½ cup Kalamata olives
- 1 tsp capers
- ½ cup olive oil
- 1 tablespoon balsamic vinegar

DIRECTIONS

1. In a bowl chop olive and mix with crushed garlic
2. Add the rest of ingredients and mix well
3. Chill for 1-2 hours serve with asparagus or vegetables

Serves: **2**

Prep Time: **10** Minutes

Cook Time: **20** Minutes

Total Time: **30** Minutes

INGREDIENTS

- ½ lb. asparagus
- 1 tablespoon olive oil
- ½ red onion
- 2 eggs
- ¼ tsp salt
- 2 oz. cheddar cheese
- 1 garlic clove
- ¼ tsp dill

DIRECTIONS

1. In a bowl whisk eggs with salt and cheese
2. In a frying pan heat olive oil and pour egg mixture
3. Add remaining ingredients and mix well
4. Serve when ready

TOMATO FRITATTA

Serves: **2**

Prep Time: **10** Minutes

Cook Time: **20** Minutes

Total Time: **30** Minutes

INGREDIENTS

- 1 tablespoon olive oil
- ½ red onion
- 2 eggs
- ¼ tsp salt
- 2 oz. cheddar cheese
- 1 garlic clove
- ¼ tsp dill
- 1 cup tomato

DIRECTIONS

1. In a bowl whisk eggs with salt and cheese
2. In a frying pan heat olive oil and pour egg mixture
3. Add remaining ingredients and mix well
4. Serve when ready

KALE FRITATTA

Serves: **2**
Prep Time: **10** Minutes

Cook Time: **20** Minutes

Total Time: **30** Minutes

INGREDIENTS

- **1 cup kale**
- **1 tablespoon olive oil**
- **½ red onion**
- **2 eggs**
- **¼ tsp salt**
- **2 oz. cheddar cheese**
- **1 garlic clove**
- **¼ tsp dill**

DIRECTIONS

1. **In a bowl whisk eggs with salt and cheese**
2. **In a frying pan heat olive oil and pour egg mixture**
3. **Add remaining ingredients and mix well**
4. **Serve when ready**

TURNIP FRITATTA

Serves: **2**

Prep Time: **10** Minutes

Cook Time: **20** Minutes

Total Time: **30** Minutes

INGREDIENTS

- 1 cup turnip
- 2 eggs
- 1 tablespoon olive oil
- ½ red onion
- ¼ tsp salt
- 2 oz. parmesan cheese
- 1 garlic clove
- ¼ tsp dill

DIRECTIONS

1. In a bowl whisk eggs with salt and cheese
2. In a frying pan heat olive oil and pour egg mixture
3. Add remaining ingredients and mix well
4. Serve when ready

SWISS CHARD FRITATTA

Serves: **2**
Prep Time: **10**   Minutes

Cook Time: **20**   Minutes

Total Time: **30**   Minutes

INGREDIENTS

- 1 tablespoon olive oil
- ½ red onion
- ¼ cup swiss chard
- ¼ tsp salt
- 2 oz. cheddar cheese
- 1 garlic clove
- ¼ tsp dill

DIRECTIONS

1. In a bowl whisk eggs with salt and cheese
2. In a frying pan heat olive oil and pour egg mixture
3. Add remaining ingredients and mix well
4. Serve when ready

Serves: **1**
Prep Time: **5** Minutes

Cook Time: **15** Minutes

Total Time: **20** Minutes

INGREDIENTS

- 2 slices bread
- 1 cup hummus
- 1 cup sauerkraut
- 1 avocado

DIRECTIONS

1. Spread sauerkraut, avocado and hummus in each bread slice
2. Place the sandwich in a baking dish and bake at 325 F for 5-6 minutes
3. When crispy remove from the oven and serve

LETTUCE WRAPS WITH TROUT

Serves: **4**

Prep Time: **10**   Minutes

Cook Time: **30**   Minutes

Total Time: **40**   Minutes

INGREDIENTS

- 1 carrot
- ¼ cucumber
- ¼ cup shallots
- ¼ cup jalapeno
- 1 tablespoon sugar
- 1 tablespoon fish sauce
- 1 cup tomatoes
- 10 oz. smoked trout fillets
- ¼ cup basil leaves
- ¼ cup chili sauce
- ¼ cup roasted peanuts
- lettuce leaves

DIRECTIONS

1. In a bowl add shallots, fish sauce, sugar and mix well
2. Add the trout fillets and tomatoes to the marinade and toss well
3. Arrange lettuce leaves on a plate and place the trout fillets with the remaining ingredients
4. Serve when ready

Serves: 2
Prep Time: 5   Minutes

Cook Time: 15   Minutes

Total Time: 20   Minutes

INGREDIENTS

- 2 tablespoons olive oil
- 1 onion
- 1 cup almond milk
- 1 tsp curry powder
- 1 lb. shrimp
- 1 cup cauliflower

DIRECTIONS

1. In a skillet heat olive oil and sauté onion and cauliflower until soft
2. Add almond milk, curry powder, shrimp and cook until shrimp is cooked
3. When ready remove from the skillet and serve

Serves: *4-6*
Prep Time: *10*   Minutes

Cook Time: *20*   Minutes

Total Time: *30*   Minutes

INGREDIENTS

- 1 tin salmon
- 1 onion
- 1 lb. polenta
- ½ lb. flour
- 1 cup olive oil
- 1 green pepper
- 1 tsp salt

DIRECTIONS

1. In a bowl combine green peppers, onion and salmon
2. Season with salt and roll salmon into a bowl with polenta and flour
3. Place the salmon patties in a frying pan and fry until golden brown
4. When ready remove from the pan and serve

SALMON FISH CAKES

Serves:	**4-6**
Prep Time:	**10** Minutes
Cook Time:	**20** Minutes
Total Time:	**30** Minutes

INGREDIENTS

- ½ lb. salmon fillets
- 1 lb. mashed potato
- 1 handful of parsley
- ¼ lb. peas
- 1 tablespoon olive oil

DIRECTIONS

1. In a frying pan fry salmon fillets until golden brown
2. Mash the potato, add peas and parsley and mix well
3. Add salmon to the mashed potato mixture and mix everything together
4. Form patties and fry each one for 2-3 minutes
5. When ready remove from skillet

Serves: **3-4**
Prep Time: **10**   Minutes

Cook Time: **20**   Minutes

Total Time: **30**   Minutes

INGREDIENTS

- 2 delicata squashes
- 2 tablespoons olive oil
- 1 tsp curry powder
- 1 tsp salt

DIRECTIONS

1. Preheat the oven to 400 F
2. Cut everything in half lengthwise
3. Toss everything with olive oil and place onto a prepared baking sheet
4. Roast for 18-20 minutes at 400 F or until golden brown
5. When ready remove from the oven and serve

BRUSSELS SPROUT CHIPS

Serves: **2**
Prep Time: **10** Minutes

Cook Time: **20** Minutes

Total Time: **30** Minutes

INGREDIENTS

- 1 lb. brussels sprouts
- 1 tablespoon olive oil
- 1 tablespoon parmesan cheese
- 1 tsp garlic powder
- 1 tsp seasoning

DIRECTIONS

1. Preheat the oven to 425 F
2. In a bowl toss everything with olive oil and seasoning
3. Spread everything onto a prepared baking sheet
4. Bake for 8-10 minutes or until crisp
5. When ready remove from the oven and serve

Serves: *2*
Prep Time: *10*   Minutes

Cook Time: *20*   Minutes

Total Time: *30*   Minutes

INGREDIENTS

- 1 lb. carrot
- 1 tablespoon olive oil
- 1 tablespoon parmesan cheese
- 1 tsp garlic powder
- 1 tsp seasoning

DIRECTIONS

1. Preheat the oven to 425 F
2. In a bowl toss everything with olive oil and seasoning
3. Spread everything onto a prepared baking sheet
4. Bake for 8-10 minutes or until crisp
5. When ready remove from the oven and serve

BEET CHIPS

Serves: **2**
Prep Time: **10**   Minutes

Cook Time: **20**   Minutes

Total Time: **30**   Minutes

INGREDIENTS

-   1 lb. beet
-   1 tablespoon olive oil
-   1 tablespoon parmesan cheese
-   1 tsp garlic powder
-   1 tsp seasoning

DIRECTIONS

1. **Preheat the oven to 425 F**
2. **In a bowl toss everything with olive oil and seasoning**
3. **Spread everything onto a prepared baking sheet**
4. **Bake for 8-10 minutes or until crisp**
5. **When ready remove from the oven and serve**

Serves: *2*
Prep Time: *10*   Minutes

Cook Time: *20*   Minutes

Total Time: *30*   Minutes

INGREDIENTS

- 1 lb. parsnip
- 1 tablespoon olive oil
- 1 tablespoon parmesan cheese
- 1 tsp garlic powder
- 1 tsp seasoning

DIRECTIONS

1. Preheat the oven to 425 F
2. In a bowl toss everything with olive oil and seasoning
3. Spread everything onto a prepared baking sheet
4. Bake for 8-10 minutes or until crisp
5. When ready remove from the oven and serve

Serves: *2*
Prep Time: *10* Minutes

Cook Time: *20* Minutes

Total Time: *30* Minutes

INGREDIENTS

- 1 lb. radish
- 1 tablespoon olive oil
- 1 tablespoon parmesan cheese
- 1 tsp garlic powder
- 1 tsp seasoning

DIRECTIONS

1. Preheat the oven to 425 F
2. In a bowl toss everything with olive oil and seasoning
3. Spread everything onto a prepared baking sheet
4. Bake for 8-10 minutes or until crisp
5. When ready remove from the oven and serve

Serves: **2**
Prep Time: **10** Minutes

Cook Time: **20** Minutes

Total Time: **30** Minutes

INGREDIENTS

- 1 lb. taro
- 1 tablespoon olive oil
- 1 tablespoon parmesan cheese
- 1 tsp garlic powder
- 1 tsp seasoning

DIRECTIONS

1. Preheat the oven to 425 F
2. In a bowl toss everything with olive oil and seasoning
3. Spread everything onto a prepared baking sheet
4. Bake for 8-10 minutes or until crisp
5. When ready remove from the oven and serve

Serves: **2**
Prep Time: **10** Minutes

Cook Time: **20** Minutes

Total Time: **30** Minutes

INGREDIENTS

- ½ lb. garlic
- 1 tablespoon olive oil
- 1 tablespoon parmesan cheese
- 1 tsp garlic powder
- 1 tsp seasoning

DIRECTIONS

1. Preheat the oven to 425 F
2. In a bowl toss everything with olive oil and seasoning
3. Spread everything onto a prepared baking sheet
4. Bake for 8-10 minutes or until crisp
5. When ready remove from the oven and serve

Serves: *2*
Prep Time: *10* Minutes

Cook Time: *20* Minutes

Total Time: *30* Minutes

INGREDIENTS

- 1 lb. spinach
- 1 tablespoon olive oil
- 1 tablespoon parmesan cheese
- 1 tsp garlic powder
- 1 tsp seasoning

DIRECTIONS

1. Preheat the oven to 425 F
2. In a bowl toss everything with olive oil and seasoning
3. Spread everything onto a prepared baking sheet
4. Bake for 8-10 minutes or until crisp
5. When ready remove from the oven and serve

PASTA

SIMPLE SPAGHETTI

Serves: **2**
Prep Time: **5**   Minutes

Cook Time: **15**   Minutes

Total Time: **20**   Minutes

INGREDIENTS

- 10 oz. spaghetti
- 2 eggs
- ½ cup parmesan cheese
- 1 tsp black pepper
- Olive oil
- 1 tsp parsley
- 2 cloves garlic

DIRECTIONS

1. In a pot boil spaghetti (or any other type of pasta), drain and set aside
2. In a bowl whish eggs with parmesan cheese
3. In a skillet heat olive oil, add garlic and cook for 1-2 minutes
4. Pour egg mixture and mix well
5. Add pasta and stir well

6. When ready garnish with parsley and serve

PASTA WITH OLIVES AND TOMATOES

Serves: *2*
Prep Time: *5*   Minutes

Cook Time: *15* Minutes

Total Time: *20* Minutes

INGREDIENTS

- 8 oz. pasta
- 3 tablespoons olive oil
- 2 cloves garlic
- 5-6 anchovy fillets
- 2 cups tomatoes
- 1 cup olives
- ½ cup basil leaves

DIRECTIONS

1. In a pot boil spaghetti (or any other type of pasta), drain and set aside
2. Place all the ingredients for the sauce in a pot and bring to a simmer
3. Add pasta and mix well
4. When ready garnish with parmesan cheese and serve

SALAD

CHICKEN SALAD

Serves: *1*
Prep Time: *5*   Minutes

Cook Time: *5*   Minutes

Total Time: *10* Minutes

INGREDIENTS

- 2 cups cooked chicken breast
- 1 cup mayonnaise
- 1 tsp paprika
- 1 cup celery
- 1 green onion
- ¼ cup green bell pepper
- 1 cup pecans

DIRECTIONS

1. In a bowl mix all ingredients and mix well
2. Serve with dressing

TUNA SALAD

Serves: *1*
Prep Time: 5   Minutes

Cook Time: 5   Minutes

Total Time: *10*   Minutes

INGREDIENTS

- 1 egg
- 1 can tuna
- 2 tablespoons mayonnaise
- 2 stalks celery
- Pinch of salt

DIRECTIONS

1. In a bowl combin all ingredients together and mix well
2. Serve with dressing

Serves: **1**

Prep Time: **5** Minutes

Cook Time: **5** Minutes

Total Time: **10** Minutes

INGREDIENTS

- ¼ cup apple cider vinegar
- ¼ cup vegetable oil
- ¼ tsp paprika
- ¼ cup almonds
- 1-quart strawberries
- 1 romaine lettuce

DIRECTIONS

1. In a bowl combin all ingredients together and mix well
2. Serve with dressing

Serves: *1*
Prep Time: **5**   Minutes

Cook Time: **5**   Minutes

Total Time: *10*   Minutes

INGREDIENTS

- **4 beets**
- **2 tablespoons balsamic vinegar**
- **1 tsp maple syrup**
- **¼ cup tomatoes**
- **¼ cup cucumber**

DIRECTIONS

1. **In a bowl combin all ingredients together and mix well**
2. **Serve with dressing**

Serves: *1*
Prep Time: *5*   Minutes

Cook Time: *5*   Minutes

Total Time: *10*   Minutes

INGREDIENTS

- ½ cabbage
- ¼ red onion
- 1 carrot
- 1 tablespoon cilantro
- ¼ lemon

DIRECTIONS

1. In a bowl combin all ingredients together and mix well
2. Serve with dressing

PASTA SALAD

Serves: **1**
Prep Time: **5**   Minutes

Cook Time: **5**   Minutes

Total Time: **10** Minutes

INGREDIENTS

- 1 package fusilli pasta
- 2 cups tomatoes
- ¼ cup cheese
- ¼ lb. salami
- 1 green bell pepper
- 1 can black olives
- 1 can salad dressing

DIRECTIONS

1. In a bowl combin all ingredients together and mix well
2. Serve with dressing

Serves: *1*

Prep Time: 5   Minutes

Cook Time: 5   Minutes

Total Time: *10*   Minutes

INGREDIENTS

- 2 cucumber
- 1 cup feta cheese
- 1 cup olive
- ¼ cup red onion
- 1 tablespoon olive oil

DIRECTIONS

1. In a bowl combin all ingredients together and mix well
2. Serve with dressing

SPINACH SALAD

Serves: **1**
Prep Time: **5**   Minutes

Cook Time: **5**   Minutes

Total Time: **10**   Minutes

INGREDIENTS

- ¼ cup almonds
- 1 lb. spinach
- 1 cup cranberries
- 1 tablespoon sesame seeds
- ¼ tsp paprika
- ¼ cup apple cider vinegar

DIRECTIONS

1. In a bowl combin all ingredients together and mix well
2. Serve with dressing

Serves: **1**
Prep Time: **5**   Minutes

Cook Time: **5**   Minutes

Total Time: **10** Minutes

INGREDIENTS

- 10 oz. black beans
- 10 oz. corn kernels
- 10 oz. kidney beans
- 1 green bell pepper
- 1 red bell pepper
- 1 red onion
- ¼ cup olive oil
- 1 tablespoon lime juice
- ¼ tsp chili powder

DIRECTIONS

1. In a bowl combin all ingredients together and mix well
2. Serve with dressing

THANK YOU FOR READING THIS BOOK!

CPSIA information can be obtained
at www.ICGtesting.com
Printed in the USA
BVHW071211180321
602885BV00007B/764